ARCTIC WILDLIFE

BY DIANE BAILEY

ARCTIC WILDLIFE

BY DIANE BAILEY

MASON CREST

Mason Crest
450 Parkway Drive, Suite D
Broomall, PA 19008
www.masoncrest.com

First printing
1 3 5 7 9 8 6 4 2

Series ISBN: 978-1-4222-3863-9
ISBN: 9978-1-4222-3867-7
ebook ISBN: 978-1-4222-7922-9

Library of Congress Cataloging-in-Publication Data
Names: Bailey, Diane, 1966-
Title: Arctic wildlife / by Diane Bailey.
Description: Broomall, PA : Mason Crest, [2018] | Series: Exploring the polar regions today | Includes index.
Identifiers: LCCN 2017003634| ISBN 9781422238677 (hardback) | ISBN 9781422238639 (series) | ISBN 9781422279229 (ebook)
Subjects: LCSH: Animals--Arctic regions--Juvenile literature. | Ecology--Arctic regions--Juvenile literature.
Classification: LCC QL105 .B344 2018 | DDC 591.9989--dc23 LC record available at https://lccn.loc.gov/2017003634

Developed and Produced by Shoreline Publishing Group.
Developmental Editor: James Buckley, Jr.
Design: Tom Carling, Carling Design Inc.
Production: Sandy Gordon
www.shorelinepublishing.com
Front cover: Dreamstime.com: Iakov Filiminov.

QR Codes disclaimer:

CONTENTS

Key Icons to Look For

 Words to Understand: These words with their easy-to-understand definitions will increase the reader's understanding of the text, while building vocabulary skills.

 Sidebars: This boxed material within the main text allows readers to build knowledge, gain insights, explore possibilities, and broaden their perspectives by weaving together additional information to provide realistic and holistic perspectives.

 Educational Videos: Readers can view videos by scanning our QR codes, providing them with additional educational content to supplement the text. Examples include news coverage, moments in history, speeches, iconic moments, and much more!

 Text-Dependent Questions: These questions send the reader back to the text for more careful attention to the evidence presented here.

 Research Projects: Readers are pointed toward areas of further inquiry connected to each chapter. Suggestions are provided for projects that encourage deeper research and analysis.

 Series Glossary of Key Terms: This back-of-the-book glossary contains terminology used throughout this series. Words found here increase the reader's ability to read and comprehend higher-level books and articles in this field.

INTRODUCTION

Nothing lives right at the North Pole. The pole is actually in the middle of the Arctic Ocean, so even Santa and Rudolph would need a houseboat! But the area surrounding the pole—the Arctic Circle—is home to some amazing wildlife. These animals have to be hardy and strong. In the cold climate and harsh terrain of the Arctic, survival is a challenge.

The Arctic Circle is an imaginary line drawn around the very top of the globe. Imagine if you took a (very small) saucer and placed it on top of a (very large) beach ball—that's about what the area inside the Arctic Circle looks like. The Arctic region, however, is not really a circle. Scientists usually define the Arctic as the area north of the tree line—the farthest northern point where trees are able to grow. In some areas this extends south of the Arctic Circle, and in other places stops north of it.

Polar bears are at the top of the Arctic food chain, but their future is more and more in doubt because of climate change.

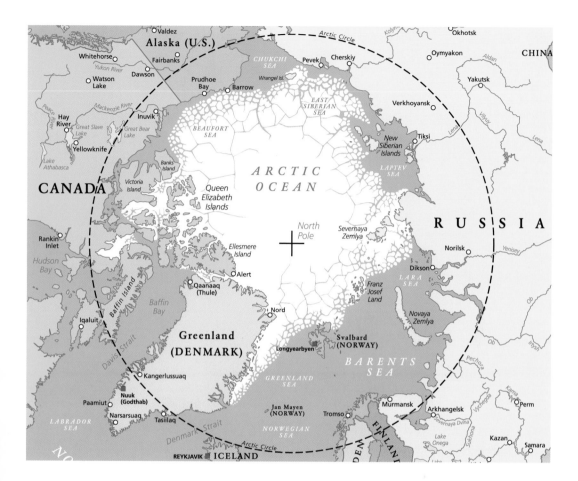

The animals that live in the Arctic have evolved with specific ways to deal with the Arctic climate. Some thrive in the ice and sea closest to the North Pole. Others depend on the more fertile tundra, the open plains south of the ice where grasses and other plants grow.

Historically, the Arctic environment was too severe to support many people. But as the world becomes more industrialized and populated, human activity is increasing in the Arctic. Big companies and national governments are pushing in. They hope to cash in on the area's natural resources, from huge stocks of fish to vast reserves of underground oil. It puts a lot of pressure on this delicate environment. Global warming is also taking a toll, melting the ice caps at a record pace. Although the Arctic has a wealth of wildlife—if you know where to look— these animals face major challenges in the coming decades.

Powerful and uniquely adapted to life in a harsh climate, polar bears are the most famous of the many types of animals that live above the Arctic Circle.

Polar Bears

1

Words to Understand

apex predator   an animal at the top of the food chain, with no natural enemies

buoyancy   an ability to float

camouflaged   to be disguised by blending in with the surroundings

carnivore   an animal that eats mostly (or entirely) other animals

floe   a large sheet of ice floating on the water

metabolism   the process the body uses to break down food and get energy from it

There's no question that polar bears are the mightiest animals in the Arctic. And there's no question how they got that reputation. They have the stamina to swim for hours and walk hundreds of miles. They can crush seals to death with a squeeze of their huge paws, and scare off any challengers with a menacing growl. They are **apex predators** in the Arctic, and everyone down the line knows it!

Land and Sea

Scientifically speaking, polar bears are marine mammals, because they rely on the sea for food. However, they are just as comfortable on land. The Arctic landscape can be a stingy one, especially in winter, but these massive **carnivores** are used to covering large territories in order to get enough food. Scientists observed one polar bear whose range was more than 60,000 square miles (155,000 sq km). That's an area about the size of the state of Georgia.

A polar bear's body is perfectly adapted to the Arctic environment. Other types of bears have thick shoulders and large heads, but the polar bear is the opposite. It's got a slender head to make it more streamlined for swimming. It also makes it easier to stick its head into small holes in the ice to catch prey. Its paws, however, are as big as dinner plates. A polar bear's large feet work like paddles in the water. On the ice they act like snowshoes, helping to distribute the animal's weight more evenly, so it is less likely to break through thin ice.

Polar bears look white, but in fact, their fur is made of hollow, colorless hairs. The air inside the hair scatters light and makes the hairs look white, so the bears stay **camouflaged** against the snow. When polar bears get dirty or have a lot of oil in their hair, they look more cream-colored or yellow. They've also got two layers of fur. The undercoat, closest to their skin, is called ground hair. It's about 2 inches (5 cm) long, and provides a layer of warmth. The outer layer is made up of guard hairs. They are

Even as humans encroach more and more into their habitat, polar bears still have room to roam—and swim—for now.

longer, reaching 6 inches (15 cm), and the air inside provides insulation and **buoyancy** for long swims across the water. Underneath the skin is a layer of blubber, or fat, that's 2–6 inches (5–15 cm) thick, providing even more warmth and buoyancy.

In short, a polar bear is unlikely to get cold. Only in the most extreme weather will a polar bear take shelter in an underground den dug into the snow. In fact, the main danger for polar bears

Polar bears are surprisingly agile for their size. Though they are good, strong swimmers, they would prefer to move on land. Ice that is breaking up makes that harder.

is getting too hot. If that happens, they can take a quick swim to cool them off, or roll onto their backs, legs splayed out in the air, to lose heat through their feet and inner thighs.

Walk, Don't Run

Polar bears may look like they're lazy, lumbering along in no hurry at all. Given that they're at the top of the food chain, they usually don't have to run *from* anything—only *after* their prey! If necessary, a polar bear can run up to 25 mph (40 kph) for a short period of time, but their normal pace is much slower, about 3.4 mph (5.5 kph). There's a reason for that. Compared to other animals, polar bears need much more energy per pound to move. The faster they go, the more energy it takes.

Slow going also keeps their body temperature lower. A polar bear's normal body temperature is about the same as a human's: 98.6°F (37°C). And when the temperature is a pleasant –10°F (–23°C) or so, they can stay cool as long as they stroll slowly. If they pick up the pace, though, their body temperature climbs fast—and so does the amount of energy they use up. Polar bears instinctively know this. One researcher devised a polar bear treadmill. After he taught a bear how to use it, he experimented by putting the bear through its paces at different speeds. If the treadmill speed was set too fast, the bear got off or simply lay down and refused to walk. It didn't like when the pace was too slow, either. Then he growled in displeasure. He seemed to know the exact speed that was most efficient.

Seals and birds make up most of the polar bears' diet. They need the fatty blubber from these animals for energy and to build weight to survive the winter.

The Hunt

At roughly 1,000 pounds (454 kg), polar bears are the Earth's largest land carnivore. Other species of bears eat lots of plants, but in the Arctic, there isn't enough vegetation to support a polar bear's weight. Plus, the chilly weather means that polar bears need a high-calorie, high-fat diet. Seals are usually the main course—and it's the seals' fat that the bears want. In fact, they'll often eat *only* the fat, and leave the meat behind for other Arctic animals to scavenge.

The ringed seal is the polar bear's favorite meal. These seals hang out around large ice **floes** several miles out into the ocean. Polar bears swim out to the ice floes, and sniff out holes in the ice where the seals come up for air. (Polar bears have an excellent sense of smell. They can sniff out prey from 18 miles/29 km away, and are able to find seals even when they're hiding under 3 feet/1 m of snow or ice.) The bears have to be patient. Sometimes they have to keep watch for days. But when the seals emerge, the bears are ready. Their massive claws dig into the seal's neck, and pull it out of the water for the kill. But it's worth the wait—a polar bear can eat 100 pounds (45 kg) of fat during a single meal, enough for several days.

Tooling Around

Polar bears are smart animals. Biologists believe their intelligence could match that of apes— roughly the same as a 3-year-old human. That might not seem very smart, but it's enough to outsmart a seal. Polar bears are also able to walk upright, on two legs. Their forelegs can then act like arms, so they can pick up objects. Only a few animals have shown the ability to use tools, and polar bears are one of them. Polar bears in zoos have figured out that they can use sticks or other objects to knock down food that has been hung out of their reach. They can also climb on barrels or other platforms and use them as stairs to get to higher places. It's much more difficult to study polar bears in the wild, but there are some reports polar bears use tools there, as well. Explorers from the 19th century told stories of polar bears throwing chunks of ice at walruses to knock them out, so the bears could go in for the kill. Biologists today have not witnessed that behavior firsthand, but some think it's certainly possible.

If seals aren't available, polar bears may decide to attack a young or weak walrus. They might also snack on birds or a hare, but only if they are easy to catch. A chase lasting more than a few seconds would require too much energy for what the bear gets back.

Especially during winter, there's not much fresh water available in the Arctic, but polar bears have also adapted to this. As their

Polar bear cubs stay with their mother for two to three years, nursing and learning the skills they need to survive on their own.

bodies break down fat through the process of **metabolism**, they produce water as a byproduct. The polar bear's body reabsorbs the water. That way, it does not get dehydrated.

Usually, polar bears are solitary animals. They hunt and eat alone. However, occasionally they'll get together for a group dinner. When there's a large meal available—such as the carcass of an adult walrus or a beluga whale—there's plenty to go around, and several polar bears will gather and share the food.

The Ice

The life of a polar bear is closely tied to the ice. It lives and travels on huge patches of ice that form in the Arctic Ocean. But survival is becoming more difficult. Most scientists agree that the Earth's climate is changing. Global warming is pushing up worldwide temperatures. The three years between 2014 and 2016 all set records for the hottest years ever. The coldest areas of the planet—the polar regions—are even more affected by global warming. As the temperature rises in the Arctic, the ice is melting at a record pace. The polar bears have less and less ice to travel on, and it's a longer swim from one ice floe to the next.

Polar bears can handle a swim of 50 miles (80 km) or so, increasing it to 200 miles (320 km) is pushing it. Worse, these desperate swims may occur when polar bears are already hungry and weakened, cutting their

The state of polar bears

odds for survival. In recent years, researchers have seen many more polar bears that are smaller and skinnier. The scientists are worried that the overall health of the polar bears is declining.

Climate change is the polar bear's biggest obstacle, but there are other threats to their habitat, as well. In recent years, there has been a push to use natural resources found in the Arctic. For example, it's estimated that about 15–30 percent of the world's oil and natural gas is beneath the Arctic, either under the ice or the seabed. Several countries, including the United States, Russia, and Norway, are considering drilling for this oil. If they do, it could be extremely hard on the polar bears' habitat.

Polar bears travel a long way each year in their search for food. They don't understand national boundaries, so it's up to people from all the Arctic countries to come together to help them.

 Text-Dependent Questions:

1. What is one advantage of polar bears having big feet?
2. How do polar bears get enough water?
3. What is a polar bear's favorite meal?

 Research Project

Global warming is a big threat to polar bears. How do scientists think rising temperatures will affect the Arctic in the next 30 years? What will the consequences be for polar bears?

Polar Bear City

Polar bears tend to be solitary animals, but there's one place in Canada that's like a polar bear restaurant and recreation center rolled into one. About a thousand bears show up each year in Churchill, Manitoba, in Canada. Thousands of tourists go there, too, hoping to catch an up-close glimpse of these magnificent animals. Travelers pile into special "tundra buggies" and head out onto the ice to see the bears in their natural habitat. They may also spot them in the town itself. The bears have figured out Churchill's garbage dump is a great snack bar, and the locals have gotten used to living with their furry visitors. Signs warn people to "Bear Aware," especially at night, and there's a "polar bear patrol" that makes sure curious polar bears don't get too close. The ones that are particularly troublesome get hauled off to "polar bear jail," where they have to cool their heels for a month. They don't get any food, only water, to make sure they don't enjoy themselves too much and come back for another stay!

The waters around the Arctic Circle are home to a huge array of marine mammals that are drawn to the rich, cold waters.

Marine Mammals

2

Words to Understand

baleen   a filtering system found in the mouths of some whales, used to separate food from seawater

echolocation   a way that animals can use sound echoes to find objects

ecosystem   the places that species live, and how they interact with each other and their environment

plankton   plants and animals, usually very small, that cannot swim and provide food for many larger animals

Sitting at the top of the world, the Arctic Ocean is known for a couple of things. One is obvious—it's cold! The other is that it has an abundance of life. That might seem strange given the temperature, but the animals that live there like it that way. Plus, the waters are full of food. The Arctic Ocean is the final destination for many river systems in North America and Russia. The rivers collect nutrients, and then carry them north and deposit them into the Arctic. This creates an environment that is hospitable for all kinds of life, from tiny microorganisms on up to jumbo-sized marine mammals.

Whales

Whales are massive creatures with lots of body fat to keep them warm, so they're right at home in chilly Arctic water. Several species of whales live in the Arctic at least part of the year, and three of them call it their home all year long. Bowhead, beluga, and narwhal whales rarely travel south of the Arctic Circle.

Bowheads: Bowhead whales are a type of **baleen** whale. Baleen is sometimes called whalebone, but it's actually made from keratin, the same substance in hair and fingernails. In baleen whales, the upper jaws are fitted with a number of baleen plates that have a fringe on the bottom. The fringe acts like a filter system. Water passes through the fringe, but food gets trapped. Whales can feed just by swimming around with their mouths open! It's okay if it takes awhile—bowheads can survive for a year without food.

Bowheads can grow 60 feet (18.3 m) long and weigh 60 tons (54 tonnes). Their heads are incredibly long, stretching back to about a third of their entire body length. That's about the height of a two-story building. Bowheads are believed to live very long lives, perhaps as long as 200 years. That may be because of the cold environment of the Arctic. Physical development is slow—after all, it takes a while to build up a layer of blubber that's a foot-and-a-half (0.5 m) thick! This also leads to a slower reproductive cycle. By evolving to live longer, they have a better chance of mating.

Belugas are among the most unique looking whales, and among the world's most vocal. This captive beluga gives a good look at the open mouth that makes those sounds.

Like all mammals, bowhead whales have to breathe air, but they can swim underwater for 15 minutes or so before they need to surface. In the Arctic, they are swimming beneath ice a lot of the time, so if they can't find a patch of open water, they simply break a hole through the ice with their heads. They look for "thin" ice, but to a bowhead, this can mean 2 feet (.6 meters) thick!

Belugas: Bowheads may have big mouths, but it's the beluga whale that likes to make itself heard. Belugas are sometimes called "canaries of the sea" because they make a lot of vocalizations. They sound like squeaks, clicks, whistles, and ringing bells.

As this beluga whale rolls over to dive after surfacing for a breath of air—as all marine mammals do—it reveals a lack of a dorsal fin, an adaptation for Arctic survival.

They make these sounds in the process of **echolocation**, which helps them find food. Belugas are not baleen whales. Instead, they belong to a group called toothed whales. Instead of dining solely on **plankton** and other tiny organisms, belugas eat a variety of fish, as well.

Many whales and dolphins have a dorsal fin on their backs, which helps keep them stable in the water. Not the beluga. A dorsal fin would add surface area to its body, which means losing more heat—not a great idea in the Arctic! Also, the lack of a fin lets the whales travel just under the surface of the ice as they look for breathing holes. A dorsal fin would scrape on the ice and get in the way. However, belugas do have a dorsal ridge along the rear half of their backs. This line of rigid, knobby bumps can be used to poke holes in the ice to make breathing holes.

Narwhals: If narwhals could talk, the first question scientists might ask is, "What is that tusk for?" Narwhals live exclusively in the Arctic, and are easily identified because they have a long, thin, spiraling ivory tusk that protrudes from the front of their heads. The tusks can be very long; on older males, they can reach 10 feet (3 m) long. (These tusks probably washed ashore at some point and started the legend of unicorns.)

The long, hard horn at the front of the narwhal's head is visible as this small pod surfaces. Scientists are not sure what the horn is for.

There are lots of ideas about why the narwhal has a tusk. Maybe it was used as a way to attract mates, or to fight other animals. It's also been suggested the tusk was a way to poke around on the ocean floor to look for food. Scientists may have found the answer during a study conducted in 2014. They found that ocean water enters the tusk and then flows through narrow tunnels until it reaches nerve endings at the base. The nerves send signals to the brain, which then determines information about the narwhal's surroundings, such as the temperature of the water or how much salt it contains.

Even from birth, narwhals are well adapted to the Arctic environment. Newborn narwhal calves are nearly a third the size of their parents, so that they've got the body mass to withstand the cold. Polar bears and orcas (killer whales) may prey on narwhals, but these whales can generally take cover in extremely cold or deep water. They're expert divers, sometimes submerging more than a mile (1.6 km) to fill up on squid or schools of Arctic cod. They have flexible rib cages to withstand the pressure at those depths, and their muscles are chock-full of oxygen to sustain them until they can surface again.

Seals

Seals live all over the world, but only a few species, called "ice seals," have adapted well to the cold environment of the Arctic. The ribbon seal, ringed seal, harp seal, and spotted seal are all named for the distinctive patterns each one has on its coat.

Another species is the bearded seal. All seals have whiskers that actually help them find food, but these hairs are especially prominent on the bearded seal, giving it its name. The hooded seal is the largest of the Arctic species. It can grow up to 9 feet (2.7 m) long and weigh 900 pounds (408 kg). The males have an inflatable flap of skin, or hood, on their heads. They blow it up as part of their mating rituals.

Seals spend a great deal of time in the water, and their bodies are made to swim. On land they look fat and awkward, but when they stretch out they become long, thin, swimming machines. They've got two sets of flippers, one in front and one in back. The rear ones provide the power, and the front ones are for steering.

Ice seals use the ice in much the same way that seals in warmer climates use land.

Arctic Cod

About 400 species of fish live in the Arctic Ocean. Most of them tend to hang out on the ocean floor, snacking on smaller creatures that live in the sediment. The Arctic cod is different. It's a little more adventurous, swimming around in a much larger range at mid-depths. The fish isn't much to look at. It's about 10 inches (25 cm) long, with a few spots on its back and a swath of silver on its belly. A chemical in its blood acts like antifreeze, so the fish can thrive even when the temperature drops below freezing, and its protruded lower jaw lets it scrape up food from the underside of the ice. The Arctic cod is happy eating plankton, crustaceans, shrimp— and, occasionally, other members of its own species! The Arctic cod is the most common fish in the Arctic and it's a key link in the food chain. It's one of the main food sources for narwhals, belugas, ringed seals, several species of birds, and larger fish such as Greenland halibut or Atlantic salmon.

When a marine mammal climbs onto land or ice, the behavior is known as "hauling out." Here, a ringed seal takes a breather and hopes not to be swamped by a killer whale.

They come ashore to rest, shed their skins, give birth (actual mating usually happens in the water), and nurse their pups.

Walruses

Fat, flabby, and fin-footed, massive walrus don't move quickly on land, but once they slip into the water, these creatures are surprisingly fast. Scientists used to think these "gentle giants" of the Arctic were happy to dine on small animals like clams and shellfish. Now, they suspect walruses might be a little more aggressive. New evidence has shown that walruses spice up their diet by pursuing geese, ducks, and birds called murres. They'll also eat seals.

As walruses swim along the shore, usually in shallow water where shellfish are plentiful, they occasionally come to shore to rest. These haul-outs are quite a sight: Walruses are social creatures that are rarely found alone, so a haul-out can involve

A herd of walruses heads for shore, showing off long, ivory tusks and bewhiskered faces. These massive animals gather in enormous groups on Arctic shores.

hundreds of animals, all piled on top of one another. They're lazing around, but they're also ready to move at a moment's notice. They have a keen sense of smell and know when potential predators are getting too near. Even a polar bear is unlikely to attack an adult walrus, but walruses are always alert to the presence of humans, their main land predator.

Challenges to Marine Mammals

Despite their differences, there's one thing that unites marine mammals in the Arctic: They all need sea ice. Seals and walruses use the ice as rest stops in their travels. Much of the food they eat tends to live near the shores of ice. Whales never come ashore, but they also depend on the ice to create habitats for the fish and plants that they eat. Narwhals may be one of the Arctic species most in danger from climate change—even more than polar bears—since they depend on the icy waters and have a smaller range than other species.

The loss of ice corresponds to rising water temperatures from global warming. That can be dangerous for species that have evolved to live in colder temperatures. In addition, fish or mammals that are not native to the Arctic have started to move in, probably looking for relief from the global warming that's affecting their part of the world. Now they're eating up food that Arctic species used to count on. For

Canada's harp seals

Will whales continue to find enough food in the cold Arctic waters? As the world's climate changes, this region is seeing the first and strongest effects.

example, gray whales usually spend summers in the Arctic Ocean before traveling south to Mexico for the winter. Now there is evidence that they are pushing deeper into the Arctic for food, and remaining there much longer.

In short, climate change is affecting where animals live, how they migrate and travel, and what they eat. Many scientists believe that marine mammals are the first to show what's going on throughout the **ecosystem**. Keeping a close watch on their behavior may provide the best clues about what problems are getting worse—and how to solve them.

Quiet, Please!

Even in the depths of the ocean, peace and quiet can be hard to find. Sound travels easily and far underwater, so even small sounds are magnified. Although chattering whales and dolphins make some of the noise, it's actually humans—or human inventions—that make most of it. From the rumble of ship engines to the signals sent out by submarines, the water is becoming a very noisy place. Noise pollution can be very hard on marine animals. If there's too much background noise, they can't hear each other through all the racket. Loud sounds can also damage their sensitive hearing and hurt their ability to communicate and navigate. In 2008, more than 1,000 narwhals got trapped in the ice and died before they could migrate to their winter home. Experts think they were trying to avoid the noise from scientists conducting underwater experiments nearby. While ocean noise pollution is a problem all over the world, it seems to be particularly bad in the Arctic. There, sound travels farther, and closer to the surface, than it does in warmer waters. Unfortunately, that's exactly where most marine mammals spend a lot of their time. Plus, in the past, the thick layer of ice muffled the sounds traveling through the water. Now, the "sound-proof walls" are melting away.

Text-Dependent Questions:

1. What is one reason that beluga whales do not have dorsal fins?

2. Name three species of seals known as "ice seals."

3. What is one way that noise pollution harms marine mammals?

 Research Project

Many animals migrate during the year to find better feeding grounds. Find out more about one of the whale species explored in this chapter. Where and when do they migrate? Make a map showing their annual travels.

In the winter, this is a frozen wasteland. In warmer months, it is a marshy wetland. Animals of all types have found ways to adapt to both environments.

Life on the Tundra

3

Words to Understand

domesticated   a wild animal that has been tamed for people to use

indigenous   native or original to a particular place

permafrost   a layer of soil that stays frozen all year long

temperate   having mild temperatures

tundra   land where the subsoil is permanently frozen

The Arctic summer does not last long. It starts in late June, and six weeks later, by the beginning of August, autumn is on the way. During this brief time, though, the **tundra** comes alive, exploding with grasses, flowers, and wildlife. A foundation of **permafrost** lies just 3–6 feet (1–2 m) below the surface, but the shallow layer of soil on top provides food and habitat for a number of species.

Predators

Polar bears rule on the ice of the northern Arctic, but on the tundra, a few species share the load at the top levels of the food chain. Wolves, wolverines, and foxes are all predators that actively hunt other animals. However, they are versatile carnivores. When they can't find live prey, they switch to scavenging. They'll eat the remains of animals that have died naturally, or the leftovers from other animals' kills.

Wolves: Wolves are not the strongest animals (although those teeth are nothing to mess with), but they are smart. While they may hunt individually, they also come together as a team to take down large prey such as caribou, moose, or muskoxen.

With their white or light gray coloring, wolves can blend into the background, staying hidden as they patiently observe their prey. They're not afraid to speak up when necessary, though: The howl of a wild wolf is one of the most recognizable sounds in nature. The howling is not usually at the moon, but at each other. Howling lets other members of the pack know where they are, and establishes territory that outsiders won't enter.

A thousand years ago, Native Americans respected wolves and thought of them as important members of nature. Wolves could be dangerous, but they rarely attacked humans. Instead, the idea of the

Wild Russia

Wolves hunt in packs, camouflaged in the snow, and work together to bring down very large prey such as moose or caribou.

vicious wolf came after people began to raise livestock, and had to defend them from hungry wolves. Hundreds of years ago, the wolf's natural territory extended southward into Europe and Canada, but by the 16th and 17th centuries they had been driven out. Now wolves live almost exclusively in Arctic regions, where there are few people to bother them.

Foxes: Another clever carnivore is the fox. The red fox is a common animal located throughout the **temperate** zones in the northern hemisphere. They also live in the Arctic. But the Arctic

The Arctic fox can be found throughout the entire Arctic Circle. In winter it has this white coat, but changes to brown in summer to blend in with plants and brush.

fox is the region's homegrown hero. These foxes have an array of adaptations that help them manage the Arctic environment. Small noses and ears help them conserve heat, and thick white fur covers their whole body, including their feet. Their tails are particularly thick, and can be wrapped around their bodies like built-in blankets.

In the winter, Arctic foxes sometimes let polar bears do the work for them in finding food. Once a polar bear kills a seal and devours the blubber, a fox can move in to scavenge the remaining meat. Other animals want in on the seal, too, but they had better wait their turn. Over-anxious birds may not get a meal—they may become one for a fox! And if polar bears haven't gotten things started, these foxes will take down ringed seals—one of the smaller species of seals—by themselves.

Wolverines: Despite their name, these animals are closely related to weasels, not wolves, but they are certainly fierce hunters. They are aggressive and strong, with powerful jaws that can crunch through bones. Even though they may only weigh 30 pounds (13.6 kg), they'll take on much larger prey like caribou.

Wolverine, the comic-book character, took his name from this very fierce and sharp-clawed predator found in Canada and Russia, among other Arctic places.

But they're not picky: The bodies of wolverines are long and skinny, which makes it easier for them to pursue animals that live in underground burrows. Rats, Arctic hares, and marmots are among their prey.

Wolverines have adapted well to the Arctic environment. Their big paws act like snowshoes to let them travel faster, and they can build dens in the snow. They have even figured out how to make refrigerators. If they have extra food, they bury it in the snow to preserve it for later.

The Grazers

There's not always a lot to eat in the tundra, but the grazing animals that live there are very good at getting what does grow. For one thing, they're very dedicated. They'll walk for days and patiently work at digging up even tiny tufts of grass or roots.

Caribou: In North America, they're called caribou; in Russia, they're known as reindeer. Either way, these hoofed animals have mastered the tundra. A good-sized male can be 7 feet long (2.1 m) and weigh 400 pounds (181 kg), yet these animals exist on what seems to be a pretty meager diet. They'll eat leaves and grass when available, but through the winter they dine mostly on lichen. Lichen is an unusual organism, a cross between a fungus and algae. It looks a little like moss, and doesn't sound very appetizing, but it grows all over the Arctic, giving the caribou plenty of food. And if there isn't any close by, that's okay. Cari-

One of the largest animals on the tundra is the caribou, but it only survives thanks to some of the tiniest plants—various types of moss and lichen (inset).

bou are always on the move. It's not unusual for them to travel thousands of miles in a year, looking for food.

Although North American caribou only live in wild herds, in Russia some of them have been **domesticated**. Herders follow them through their yearly migrations, sometimes directing them to feeding grounds and hunting them for food as necessary.

Eaten Alive

Take your pick: Would you rather be trapped in a winter storm in the Arctic, or a summer one? The winter one is made up of snow. The summer one? Mosquitoes! The Arctic gets muggy during the spring thaw, when shallow lakes form on the tundra. There, mosquitoes breed, and swarm in huge numbers. Since there aren't a lot of food options in the Arctic, these blood suckers go after whatever they can find. Large animals like caribou have it particularly bad since they offer a large, easy meal. When mosquitoes swarm, the caribou flee to less-infested areas, trying to escape. But more time running means less time eating, and it takes a toll on them. The caribou aren't being wimpy: Sometimes they are attacked so mercilessly that they die from loss of blood. Unfortunately, scientists think that, as global warming gets worse, so will the mosquito problem.

Muskoxen: A muskox coat has two layers. The first is kind of like long underwear. It's a thin layer of wool that fits snugly all over the body. The outer coat of guard hairs is long and shaggy. The hair toward the underside of the muskox covers its legs and almost reaches the ground. The muskox looks less like an animal with a big coat, than a big coat with a head and feet! Even with a blizzard sweeping across the tundra, the muskox patiently waits it out, immune to the biting cold. In fact, it will even seek out the tops of hills—the windiest, most exposed areas—because the wind has blown away the snow and uncovered any vegetation on the ground.

There's no need for the muskox to develop white hair to camouflage itself, as some other Arctic animals do. It is strong and solid, with few natural predators. A bear might take on a weak or hurt muskox, but usually the only animals willing to attempt an attack are wolves. Even then, they'll only give it a try if they can manage to separate a skittish muskox from the rest of the herd.

A muskox shows off its distinctive horns and heavy, shaggy coat. These animals are found mostly in northern Canada and far northern Greenland.

Birds

When the tundra blooms, thousands of birds appear to take advantage of the summer bounty. It is light nearly 24 hours a day through the summer, and the Arctic tundra turns into a huge buffet. Some of the world's most impressive birds of prey, such as

Snowy owls are among the few birds that winter in the Arctic.

bald eagles and peregrine falcons, make the journey from warmer climates to feast on fish, smaller birds, and rodents.

Some birds live in the Arctic even through the dark of winter. The snowy owl is at home staying in the Arctic all year, as long as it can find food. Owls like to hunt at night anyway, so the dark doesn't bother them. The snow isn't a deterrent, either. They can sniff out a lemming that's hiding a foot (0.3 m) under the snow. When pursuing a hare, snowy owls turn into one-legged skiers: they grip their prey with one leg, and drag the other in the snow to slow down the sprinting hare.

Ptarmigans are another year-round resident of the Arctic. You expect a bird to have feathers, but ptarmigans take it to the extreme. Not only do they have feathers on the main part of their bodies, they've also got them on their feet, providing insulation and traction on slippery ice. They even have feathers inside their nostrils!

This summertime ptarmigan does not have its heavy winter feathers.

Both snowy owls and ptarmigans are great at camouflage. In the winter their feathers turn white, to blend in with the snow. Now it's a matter of luck and skill. Will the snowy owl disguise itself enough to swoop down unnoticed on the ptarmigan and get a meal? Or will the ptarmigan's white feathers keep it safely hidden? When summer comes, both species "brown up," and the contest starts again.

Future Threats

The loss of sea ice that threatens polar bears and ocean mammals is not an immediate problem for the animals that live on the tundra. There are no ships, and human traffic is minimal. Overall, their environment is more stable, but there are still concerns. The effects of climate change touch every part of the world, for example. Their food supply is in danger, too. Commercial fishermen take large amounts of fish from other parts of the Arctic. That trickles down to affect the food chain there.

One area in the tundra that gets a lot of attention is the Arctic National Wildlife Refuge, located in the northeast corner of

Stay Cool

Cold-blooded animals such as snakes and frogs don't do well in the Arctic. Unlike mammals, they cannot regulate their body temperature to stay warm even when it's cold outside. Instead, they absorb and lose heat based on the sun and the temperature of the air. When the weather's cold, so are they. But some Arctic animals have figured out a way to battle the chill. Their bodies are able to replace some of the water in their blood and cells with chemicals that don't freeze as quickly. This keeps their cells alive longer. Using this strategy, the Siberian salamander can go into a freezing state and survive temperatures as low as −49°F (−45°C). It can even stay that way for a few years. Wood frogs in Canada and Alaska have adapted in a similar way.

Visitors are welcome to explore the Arctic National Wildlife Refuge, the largest area of protected land above the Arctic Circle. It's larger than the entire state of Massachusetts.

Alaska. It is almost 20 million acres (8.1 million hectares), and is the largest wildlife preserve anywhere in the Arctic. At some point, almost all species of animals that live in the Arctic pass through. Some of them live there full-time.

Within the refuge, an area called the coastal plain, near the coast of the Beaufort Sea, is a political hot spot. Oil companies believe there could be billions of gallons of oil under the surface, and they are eager to drill for it. Many people in Alaska support this idea because it could help the economy. Environmentalists are opposed, however. They fear that drilling will tear up the coastal plain to the point it cannot recover. For example, the refuge is home to the Porcupine caribou herd, which uses the refuge as a home base to give birth to calves. The **indigenous** Gwich'in tribe in Canada depends on the herd for food. The population of the Porcupine caribou herd is stable right now, but the Gwich'in fear that drilling will disrupt their migration and permanently damage their habitat. (Read more in Chapter 4.)

The problems in the Arctic—from the northern ice down to the tundra—did not start there and do not end there. They are global issues that will require global cooperation to solve.

 # Text-Dependent Questions:

1. What animal is wolverine closely related to?

2. What is the main food for caribou?

3. For Arctic birds, what is the purpose of having feathers on the feet?

 # Research Project

Learn more about the proposals to drill for oil in the Arctic National Wildlife Refuge. What are the pros and cons? What do you think: Is it a good idea?

The search for oil has reached the Arctic. The news is good for oil companies, which have found vast reserves. The news is not so good for wildlife and the environment.

Protecting Arctic Wildlife

4

Words to Understand

drones   aircraft that carry no pilot on board and are controlled remotely

gene pool   the total amount of genes in a particular species

quota   a certain, limited amount that is determined in advance

subsistence   a basic, minimal way of living, with only things that are necessary to survive

The Arctic has a unique ecosystem—small and specialized. Many species that evolved in this environment can survive nowhere else on Earth. Now, it's a question of whether they can survive in the Arctic. There's a common thread to the problems they face: Climate change, pollution, and industrial activity are all caused by humans. The good news is that people are also taking action to stop those problems.

Protecting Polar Bears

Polar bears are a symbol of the Arctic. Scientists think there are about 20,000–25,000 polar bears worldwide, but no one knows for sure. It's difficult to count them accurately. And even though their total numbers aren't a big concern, researchers are worried that they're seeing more weak, malnourished animals. Polar bears are among the first animals to show strain from environmental changes. If they're suffering, other animals might not be far behind. In any case, biologists agree that the time to protect them is now, before it's too late.

Governments around the world have come together to help address global warming, but it will take time. In the meantime, the sea ice is melting, and every year polar bears have to travel farther to find food. Sometimes they don't make it. It's even more unfortunate when it's a female with a cub. If a cub loses its mother before it reaches two years old, it won't survive. It needs time to learn how to hunt, and needs protection from older bears while it's learning. But in the increasingly harsh world of the Arctic, sometimes the mother drowns or starves to death.

A polar bear rescue team based in Winnipeg, Manitoba, can help. If it finds a cub wandering alone, it takes it to a special facility within the Winnipeg Zoo. Now in "foster care," the cubs are introduced to zoo life and eventually the public. It's hoped that people who are able to see polar bears up close will be motivated to help the ones that live in the wild.

As polar bears need to range more widely to find food, they are crossing paths with humans. Settlements in the far north have to chase bears from trash dumps.

Polar bears in zoos are sometimes part of captive breeding programs. Captive breeding is not a good way to guard against extinction. Scientists agree that polar bears born in zoos will never learn the skills to live in the wild. However, biologists are also worried about the declining number of wild polar bears. As their numbers shrink, they become less diverse genetically. This can make them less successful at breeding in the wild. Rescued polar bears and captive breeding programs help scientists develop another **gene pool**. Those genes could be reintroduced to wild bears.

Though international whale hunting is mostly banned, exceptions are made for native people who seek to continue their traditional ways of using whales to survive.

Hunting

Traditionally, indigenous people who live in the Arctic have hunted animals as part of their **subsistence** lifestyle. Polar bears, seals, walruses, and whales were all taken. All parts of the animal were put to good use. The meat and fat were eaten for food; the skins made into clothing; the oil burned as fuel; the bones shaped into tools or used as building materials.

By the 19th century, European explorers and traders had moved into the Arctic and set up operations of their own. These commercial operations did not consider that it was important to conserve the overall numbers of the animals. Some populations of whales and seals were driven almost to extinction. It took generations for some of them to recover.

Today, hunting for whales and seals is strictly regulated in most areas. Indigenous people may continue to hunt them, as long as they only take a set number of animals. Commercial fishermen, whalers, and sealers also have **quotas**. Endangered species are off-limits.

Hunting for sport, especially of polar bears, has also been a problem. One-on-one, a person would not have a chance against the strength of a polar bear. But humans can use guns and modern technology like airplanes that lets them search for the bears over large areas.

By the middle of the 20th century, so many polar bears were being killed

Shore Leave

In Alaska and Russia, thousands of walruses haul out each season. That's just what it sounds like: They haul their huge bodies out of the water and come ashore to rest in between feedings. Walruses don't like strange sounds or smells, or unfamiliar activities. If they get spooked, the herd may stampede. Three thousand walruses multiplied by 2,000 pounds (907 kg) each equals one big wall of walrus! Young walruses can get trampled to death, and even full-grown adults can get hurt.

In places where walruses tend to gather, some communities have put rules in place to keep the walruses calm. Airplanes—especially helicopters!—are prevented from flying too low or close, because the noise disturbs the animals. People need to keep their distance, too. The scent of coffee or cologne telegraphs to a walrus that humans are nearby. That can set off a walrus, and when one starts, they all follow! Hunting is still allowed for subsistence purposes, but hunters only use traditional weapons like spears and harpoons, instead of guns that might frighten the herd.

that in the 1970s, five Arctic nations (the United States, Canada, Russia, Norway, and Denmark) entered an agreement to regulate hunting and help stabilize the polar bears' numbers. Today, it is only legal to kill bears if they are endangering people, if there is a scientific reason, or if it is by indigenous people who intend to use them as food.

The bearded seal—it can thank its whiskers for the name—was added to the endangered species list in 2016. Other Arctic species might join it.

Save the Space

Protecting habitat is probably the single most important thing to do to save Arctic animals. And, probably the single best way to do that is to slow down the effects of climate change. That will take time, and it will require cooperation from countries all over the globe. Many nations have already set goals to cut back on producing carbon dioxide, one of the gases that contributes to global warming. It's only a start, though, and if some countries don't participate, it might not work.

In the US, classifying an animal as threatened gives it extra protection. In 2008, the government determined polar bears were threatened. In 2016, bearded seals were added to the list. Part of the efforts to protect them will include preserving their habitat, and that could include measures to help climate change.

Another way to save habitat is by simply leaving it alone. Setting aside areas as preserves, and limiting or prohibiting human activity in these areas, gives animals some room to breathe. In 2016, Canada took an important step by designating an area of 911 square miles (2,361 sq km) of the ocean as protected. Not only is this particular spot popular with polar bears, seals, birds, and fish, it's also one of the main places where beluga whales spend the summer. About 40,000 show up each season— that's one-fourth of all the world's belugas.

Melting ice = trouble

People are moving through the Arctic more than ever, so setting out some ground rules for responsible travel may also help. In the past, navigating through the Arctic Ocean meant boarding a special icebreaker ship that could plow through thick ice. Parts of the Arctic still require an icebreaker, but a lot don't. So much ice has melted that a regular ship can get through. There's a lot more traffic, and it puts animals at risk. Marine mammals can be fatally struck by ships. And all animals are affected by increased pollution and interference with their habitat.

Though massive glaciers dwarf visiting cruise ships, those ships can cause real damage. Rules are in place to help people see the Arctic, but avoid problems.

In 2017, new rules went into effect for ships traveling in the Arctic. The "Polar Code" says that ships must be specially designed for Arctic travel (to reduce the chance of an accident), and that captains must plan their routes to avoid places that marine mammals are known to gather. There are also limits on how much trash or other waste they can dump into the water.

Another big issue in saving Arctic habitats concerns drilling for oil. In the past, drilling in the Arctic did not make much sense. It was hard to drill through ice to reach oil, and travel through the region was complicated and expensive. As the ice melts, though, drilling is easier, faster, and cheaper. In 2016, however, both the US and Canada banned offshore drilling in their waters. For the US, the ban was "indefinite." In Canada it would last five years and then go up for review. Environmental organizations counted the ban as a win for their cause, but there's a catch. In the US, the ban only applies to waters that are controlled

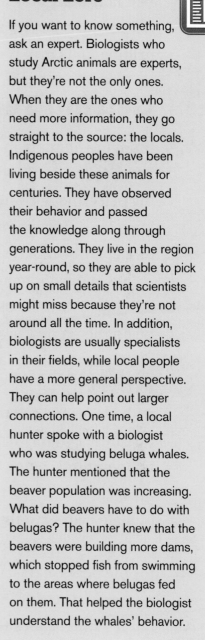

Local Lore

If you want to know something, ask an expert. Biologists who study Arctic animals are experts, but they're not the only ones. When they are the ones who need more information, they go straight to the source: the locals. Indigenous peoples have been living beside these animals for centuries. They have observed their behavior and passed the knowledge along through generations. They live in the region year-round, so they are able to pick up on small details that scientists might miss because they're not around all the time. In addition, biologists are usually specialists in their fields, while local people have a more general perspective. They can help point out larger connections. One time, a local hunter spoke with a biologist who was studying beluga whales. The hunter mentioned that the beaver population was increasing. What did beavers have to do with belugas? The hunter knew that the beavers were building more dams, which stopped fish from swimming to the areas where belugas fed on them. That helped the biologist understand the whales' behavior.

by the federal government—and that means more than 3 miles (4.8 km) from shore. Any closer than that, and the water is under the jurisdiction of the state of Alaska. The state could allow drilling in its own waters.

Getting Technical

Studying animals in the Arctic can help scientists learn more about them—and figure out ways to help them. The Arctic is a big place, though, and it's not very friendly to people who like to keep their fingers and toes warm. Following a whale, a walrus, or a polar bear across a long distance is not realistic.

Technology can help. In the past few decades, scientists have developed ways of observing animals without having to constantly be on the scene. For example, they can place electronic tags on them and then use satellites to track them. It's not always a perfect system, though. For example, currently polar bears are fitted with electronic collars that can store and transmit information, but these collars take a lot of abuse. They have to endure frigid temperatures, being plunged into saltwater, and being scraped up against ice. Also, they only work on female bears. The necks of male bears are thicker than their heads, so their collars just slide off. Now, researchers are working to develop tags—perhaps for the bears' ears—that will work better.

Aerial surveys can let scientists see a larger area more quickly, but it's still a chore to fly over the whole Arctic. Now, researchers are starting to use unmanned aerial vehicles, or **drones**, to

From an NOAA icebreaker in the Arctic Sea, a researcher sends an unmanned aircraft into flight. It will send back video and other data to help scientists.

help them do the work. They are also using better equipment. In the past, planes had to fly relatively near the ground so people looking out the window could get an accurate count. Now planes are being equipped with special sensors that detect the heat of animals' bodies, and with high-resolution cameras that snap photographs. This allows the planes to fly much higher, where they are less likely to disturb the animals.

How many more sunsets will polar bears have? Like animals around the world, they depend on human beings not to damage the habitat where they live.

Understanding Arctic animals is key to saving them, especially since we may be running out of time. The Arctic is one of the Earth's most vulnerable ecosystems. Scientists agree it's changing faster than other parts of the world, and the animals that live there cannot always change with it. What happens there depends on people all over the world. To preserve this unique region, everyone will have to work together.

Text-Dependent Questions:

1. How can keeping polar bears in zoos help those in the wild?

2. What is one rule in the "Polar Code" for ships that could help marine mammals?

3. Why do biologists like to get information from local people when studying animals?

 # Research Project

Be a biologist! Pick your favorite Arctic animal and pretend you can travel to the Arctic to study it. Choose two or three specific things you want to learn, and come up with a plan of study. What will you do?

FIND OUT MORE

Websites

www.arcodiv.org/index.html
This site has good information about the ecosystem of the Arctic Ocean. Check out the "species" section for more detailed looks into marine mammals.

naturalhistory.si.edu/arctic/html/wildlife.html
This site from the Smithsonian Institution has profiles on many of the Arctic's major species.

wwf.panda.org/what_we_do/where_we_work/arctic/wildlife/
The World Wildlife Fund works to protect species across the globe. Check out their site to find out more about Arctic animals and the efforts to protect them.

Books

Lourie, Peter. W*haling Season: A Year in the Life of an Arctic Whale Scientist.* New York: HMH Books for Young Readers, 2009.

Rosing, Norbert. *The World of the Polar Bear.* Toronto: Firefly Books, 2010.

Tarbox, A.D. *An Arctic Tundra Food Chain.* Mankato, MN: Creative Paperbacks, 2016.

Woodford, Chris. *Arctic Tundra and Polar Deserts.* Oxford, England: Raintree, 2010.

 SERIES GLOSSARY OF KEY TERMS

circumpolar: the area surrounding the North Pole, including the Arctic regions

Cold War: when nations are openly hostile toward each other while not resorting to physical warfare

continental shelf: the relatively shallow seabed surrounding a continent; the edge of a continent as it slopes down into the sea

floe: an ice sheet floating in the water

indigenous: native or original to a particular place

meteorology: the study of weather

pelts: furred animal skins

permafrost: a layer of soil that stays frozen all year long

province: an area in Canada with its own name and government, similar to a state

subsistence: a basic, minimal way of living, with only things that are necessary to survive

sustainable: something that can be maintained or practiced for a long duration without negative effects

taiga: a biome that includes the forest of mostly evergreen trees found in the southern Arctic regions

territorial waters: the parts of an ocean over which a country has control

tundra: a type of biome in very cold areas characterized by limited plant growth, frozen soil, and low rainfall

INDEX

PHOTO CREDITS

Adobe Images: Andrew Watson 6, Peter Hermes Furian 7, Volodymyr 20, Cristian Irranca 23, tryton2011 29, bmaynard 37, jmcummings88 38, Robert Kelsey 41, Segunt 41inset, G-Z Studio 42, Schaef 46, salman2 48. Alamy Stock Photo: Nature Picture Library 52. Dreamstime.com: Outdoorsman 8, 60, Ondrej Prosicky 11, 54, Vladimir Melnik 12, Vladimir Seliverstov 14, Andrey Gudkov 16, Michael Elliott 24, Anthony Hathaway 28, Luis Leamus 31, Vladimir Melnikov 34, Neil Burton 39, James Pintar 44t, Dmyrtro Pylypenko 44b, Lawrence Weslowski Jr. 56. Newscom: David Woodfall Photoshot Stock 19. NOAA: Dr. Kristin Laidre 25, Amilynn Adams 59. Shutterstock: Maksimillian 51. US Navy: 32. Wikimedia: August Linnman 27.

ABOUT THE AUTHOR

Diane Bailey has written more than 70 books for kids and teens, on everything from sports to science. Her favorite topics are history and the people who made it, and how people are trying to change the world today. Her recent books include titles about polar explorers, the fight against wildlife poachers, and rainforest conservation. She also helps other authors by editing their books. When she's not working, she likes to cook, plant flowers, and watch scary movies. Diane has two grown sons and lives in Lawrence, Kansas.

BOOK CHARGING CARD

Accession No. _____ Call No. _____

Author _____

Title _____

Date	Borrower's Name